AF442830

The Missing

Peace

Noanie Mahaney

ISBN 979-8-89243-305-1 (paperback)
ISBN 979-8-89243-306-8 (digital)

Copyright © 2024 by Noanie Mahaney

All rights reserved. No part of this publication may be reproduced, distributed, or transmitted in any form or by any means, including photocopying, recording, or other electronic or mechanical methods without the prior written permission of the publisher. For permission requests, solicit the publisher via the address below.

Christian Faith Publishing
832 Park Avenue
Meadville, PA 16335
www.christianfaithpublishing.com

Scripture quotations are all taken from the Holy Bible, New Living Translation, copyright c 1996, 2004, 2015 by Tyndale House Foundation. Used by permission of Tyndale House Publishing, Carol Stream, Illinois, 60188. All rights reserved. In his Image Devotion Bible

Printed in the United States of America

In memory of Pastor Doug Schneider
(August 1, 1952 – December 27, 2021)

Truly missing Pastor Doug's smile and his genuine warmth and good humor. Pastor Doug was a prominent person in my salvation story. I can still hear his voice, saying, "Make Jesus the center of your life." He was the pastor who prophesied over Derreck and me the first time we attended the Embassy Church. Pastor Doug is the person who gave me the understanding that God speaks to His people. Pastor Doug gave us hope and wisdom, and most of all, he was a perfect example to us of how to love others as the Lord Jesus loved.

Contents

Preface

With permission, I use the New Living Translation Bible to reference my thoughts and ideas. You will be drawn to read many different Bible translations as you grow in Christ. I recommend that you research the Word and the various divine writings of the ages. With a computer, you can compare many editions of the Holy Bible with just the click of a button. Don't be afraid to investigate the ancient sources of the biblical text, as you will understand from my writing that God gifts you with an advocate to help you decipher what is real and what is deception. Hopefully, you will invite the Holy Spirit to become your teacher in all things, and the Holy Spirit will confirm the lie or the truth in all you do when you reach that level of true understanding. I ask for a blessing over you and your family and know that there is no mistake that my story has made its way to your doorstep.

> **Look! I stand at the door and knock. If you hear my voice and open the door, I will come in, and we shall share a meal together as friends. (Revelation 3:20 NLT)**

Introduction

Deception is the work of the enemy, and today, the enemy seems to be winning souls, which is why the path to eternal life is narrow. Our world is a chaotic place, where each generation seems to morally decline further than the last. The light of hope is slowly growing dim. The enemy has infiltrated most facets of society, which means even our churches have fallen prey. In some cases, congregations attend church to be entertained rather than taught the Word of God. These same people are not getting the true biblical doctrine, which blurs the lines over time, and truth is lost.

The lack of basic knowledge of biblical texts has led potential followers away from eternal life without even understanding the error of their ways. People are being directed to believe that what they are doing in their everyday lives is righteous and that the new rules of society are God's rules, but they are not God's rules.

God is the same yesterday, today, and tomorrow. Nothing has changed, and the rules of old still apply today. If most of our population stays on the same trajectory, they will lose their souls, not even understand their choice, and think they are saved. Our government, educational system, media, advertising, and history have been manipulated and orchestrated to steer us away from God. When your eyes are opened, you will come to understand that God is slowly being erased from all of society.

I have been called to bring this to your attention. God only wants His children to make their decisions based on knowing the truth, and when deception is what they are drawing upon to decide, it makes it unfair and just plain evil. God revealed to me this problem through an exchange I had with a member of my family, and through this experience, I found that the truth has been intentionally hidden from everyone. God's children have moved so far from Him because they have been hoodwinked into thinking the Bible is not a true source of divine knowledge and that the source of divine knowledge has become the church and its pastors and reverends, who are now preaching false doctrine in some cases. Know that some are true to their teachings as well, but most churches are bending to meet the needs of the congregation and not to guide their flock through the teaching of true divine scriptures.

Churches have become what they call lukewarm, and they are not setting boundaries, and they are wishy-washy on rules because they are more concerned about what man will say or do than what God will say or do. My generation has been lied to! I hope to help set things straight and bring back the need to get back to scripture and know what it is that God wants for our lives and not what man wants for us.

My own struggle with finding salvation was long and tedious because I had to uncover the lies and deception that society presented. It took almost a lifetime for me to find the truth, and I hope that you are reading this in your younger years, as it will allow you to take the scales from your eyes much earlier than it did with me. This is my testimony to finding truth and my journey to becoming "born again." It is an honor and a blessing to share myself with you. Salvation is a gift that we need to accept with all our hearts, and when the world hides its very existence, it makes it impossible for people to move toward it at all. You are a child of God, and you deserve what is available to you, and that is the inheritance that awaits all of God's children, eternal life within the kingdom of heaven.

Chapter 1

BOLDLY EXPLAINING MYSELF

Hey, guess what? I joined a cult! Okay, okay, totally not true. But I was asked that very question when I called my sister to see how she was enjoying the Bible I gifted her for Christmas. Laughing, she replied, "That was a silly gift, Noanie."

"Pardon me?" I questioned.

Feeling blindsided, I froze in confusion. I thought to myself, *She is my sister, but we never discussed God, and I wanted to share that part of me with her.* When did society go so wrong that Christ is not even associated with Christmas? My heart sank, and a feeling of frustration and disappointment came over me.

As a new "born-again" believer, I lamely tried to explain my newfound deliverance. I babbled on about my belief in Christ Jesus and the fact that this belief had set me free. I went on to say that freedom from sin had changed my life and that I was a witness to self-transformation. The very words *born again* automatically triggered my sister to respond to me with the word *cult.* I paused and thought to myself, *Have you not read parts of the Holy Bible?* I could feel her imagination at work, churning up images of locked compounds and hypnotic doctrine. I just wanted to get off the telephone and reassess my entire approach. My explanation was fragmented and incomplete. Yikes! We said our goodbyes and hung up. It dawned on me that I was not quite prepared yet in my knowledge to present my testimony to anyone, let alone my own sister. The most transforming event of my life was something that filled my heart and soul, and I was tongue-tied.

The complexity of my adventure is profound, but the truth of it and the eventual outcome are magnificent. My only desire right now is to leap from housetop to housetop, shouting the good news of what I have discovered after fifty-seven years of searching every nook and cranny for life's answers. I now know why God presented great opposition to me through my sister.

Sister, you have inspired me to write about my journey to being "born again," and I graciously thank you! All thoughts and ideas will be referenced with the Holy Bible using the New Living Translation, as it is an easier translation to comprehend. Know that you can reference the King James Version for a more ancient translation.

I smile at God's great wisdom. God wanted me to become firm in my own understanding of our new personal relationship. The Holy Bible makes a bold statement concerning our response to others when questioned about our spiritual beliefs.

You must worship Christ as Lord of your life. And if someone asks about your Christian hope, always be ready to explain it. (1 Peter 3:15 NLT)

I chuckled to myself when I read this passage found in the Bible in the Gospel of Peter. Biblically, God uses the least likely to push His agenda, and today, His sights are set on me. Experiencing childhood poverty and family breakup has given me an unusual fear of speaking up for myself and stepping forward with my point of view. My comfort level has always been to stay in the background and work in the shadows. God seems to make us face our worst fears. Praying, I ask the Holy Spirit to be with me through this testimony as there is no way I would be able to present it alone. Well, here it goes. It's time to put all the puzzle pieces together and learn to be bold and share myself, at least on paper for now.

Chapter 2

LOST WITHOUT A CLUE

Just a few short years ago, I didn't have a clue what it meant to be saved or be a "born-again" believer. I did not understand the process, and I didn't even know there was a process. Now as I write, I regret not reading the Holy Scriptures sooner, as these answers are laid out in black-and-white on the pages of a book that is over thousands of years old and readily available to everyone—answers that were in plain sight the entire time. The enemy, Satan, has twisted the idea of following Jesus Christ into a negative or uncool way of life. Most of society has fallen away from their beliefs because of Satan's hard work and constant advertising. There is a battle going on for souls in the world today, and right now Satan appears to be winning that war.

Most people have not even picked up the Bible, which means they are relying on the interpretation of scripture by others and not their own. This leads to the spread of false doctrine and a misled and deceived society—purposely strategic and implemented as planned by the enemy himself. The evil forces of the devil have accomplished what he set out to do all along—total chaos. Satan is the master of divide and conquer. I have encountered this in my own family, whereby my parents were constantly bickering and arguing and the result of conflict is foretold in the Bible:

Similarly, a family splintered by feuding will fall apart. (Mark 3:25 NLT)

A perfect world would have handed me the scriptures at birth and allowed me full knowledge and understanding of their teachings. Unfortunately, no one hands you anything. Misinformation and lies are rampant in our society today. This evil force leads to beliefs that are based in deception and untruths, therefore shielding people from the truths of God and His real purpose for us.

Looking back, I was directed to biblical teachings. God calls us through other people, and that person for me was my mother. She often suggested I read the Holy Bible. Yes, if you heard the word *nag* when you read that sentence, you are quite right. She probably said it a thousand times. "I'll get to it, Mom," I would often say. Even the enemy tries to make us reject most of what our parents try to teach us.

Mom would say, "If you ever want to read the most fascinating book in the world, it is the Holy Bible. Every situation is presented within its pages, and the Bible is where you find the rules to life and the understanding of all things."

Our Father in heaven repeatedly makes it quite clear:

> **You must commit yourselves wholeheartedly to these commands that I am giving you today. Repeat them again and again to your children. Talk about them when you are at home and when you are on the road, when you are going to bed and when you are getting up. (Deuteronomy 6:6–7 NLT)**

Occasionally, I would sit down, turn its pages and read it, trying to understand the message it presented. The Bible seemed foreign, dated, complicated, and almost sealed off. It left me angry, frustrated, and sad, especially after reading the Book of Job. Why would God allow Satan to put Job through so much torment and loss for such a righteous man? I was baffled at the parables that Jesus would present to the crowds and I would try to decipher the one true message, but its meaning seemed to escape me. And the most difficult part of the

Bible is the last chapter called the Revelation of Jesus Christ; now that part frightened me.

The Bible even gives a blessing to all those who read Revelation and understand it:

God blesses the one who reads the words of this prophecy to the church, and he blesses all who listen to its message and obey what it says, for the time is near. (Revelation 1:3 NLT)

The Bible seemed locked and I truly tried many times to make my mom happy by opening its pages. But to no avail, I seldom did. But when I did, I was in awe of how the pages felt between my fingers and how the words seemed to emit some type of power. I knew my life would improve the moment I figured it out but, for now, it sat on the shelf.

Chapter 3

OH, NO, CHILDHOOD

Let me take you back. My childhood was broken and complicated and it would take a series of books to map it all out for you. I feel comfortable stepping out and sharing some of the details, mainly because the path to salvation is seldom smooth. I have always been a believer in learning from history and other people's mistakes, and my own should be no different when serving others.

Let me try to convey what it was like to be me in a brief explanation. My parents were both products of family dysfunction before they got together. My mother was abandoned by her father at three years of age after her mother died of poisoning. She was given away to the next-door neighbor to raise. Explain that to a three-year-old! Hence her insatiable need for both family and a strong male role model. My father was a product of sexual, physical, and mental abuse. Both of my parents were looking for an escape from unsupportive and unstructured families and came together in wedlock at the ripe old age of eighteen.

A year into the marriage, I was born, and in the next seven and a half years my mom had four more children—all girls. All my mom ever dreamed of was having a large family and her own horse. Over my school-age years, we must have moved at least once or twice a year as my parents were fascinated with the excitement and drama of the rodeo circuit. My memories consisted of Conklin midways, country music, bronco riders, calf roping, barrel racing, and constant travel. My parents were very good at what they did as my mother was a champion barrel racer and my father became a top-contending bull rider.

Since I could remember, my father and mother fought constantly. There was too much responsibility way too soon, and there was no real family foundation to draw from in the rules of a loving marriage and childcare. We were exposed to the wiles of the world while our parents tried to make a living in this unconventional way. Most holidays wound up in arguments and, as an adult, I was prone to anxiety and uneasiness with each approaching holiday or birthday.

My childhood memory brings back those times when I would lie in bed, listening to them yell and scream at each other. I would pray fervently to Jesus just to make it all stop, but it continued until my early teens. My father suffered so much from childhood abuse that he became an angry man, and he was always looking for attention from everywhere but his family. It took Mom five children to realize he wasn't changing and, by then, she understood that her need for a strong male figure in her life was not worth the tremendous effort she put into the marriage. Finally, after the verbal abuse turned into physical abuse, my mom kicked my dad out and he went, never even looking back. He left five girls under thirteen years of age without even arranging visitation or support. My mom was to maintain her livelihood, on money earned from the tips of a head waitress at a local restaurant in town.

After he left, I remember both money and food being very scarce. Most days, we ate one big meal, which would consist of potatoes, meat, and vegetables, usually cut up in a pot left on the stove, ready for us to heat up the moment we arrived home from school. There were a couple of times when I would turn on the stove, forget that it was on, and by the time I would remember, our food would be burned and inedible. Those were nights that we would put together sugar sandwiches instead, which we would be much happier eating anyway. We never felt sorry for ourselves, and we all pitched in and made the best of it. Most of the time, things seemed to pull together, even at the very last moment.

One Christmas, which still warms my heart to this day, the Salvation Army Church in our local area dropped off a large basket of food, which made Christmas so much better. There were items I had not even seen before—something called Christmas pudding wrapped in clear red wrap and bows. Wow! I was so happy.

There was another time just after dad left and mom had run out of money. She had five mouths to feed and a rodeo coming up the following weekend. She took out her checkbook and loaded us all up in the truck and trailer with her champion barrel horse, Ike. We all set out to make grocery money for the coming week. I still remember this day like it was yesterday. She tossed me a map, which I had to learn to read—one of those folded one way and then the other, confusing things. She had so much confidence in me. I was to be her copilot and I really did not have a clue what I was doing, but somehow, I was able to convey instructions on which roads to take and get us to our destination. Dad was normally the one who drove the big rig and, as I looked at my mom, she had a look of sheer determination on her face, and I knew we could do anything if we put our minds to it.

My mom must have been nervous but, in her mind, she had a job to do, and she did it. My mother had no choice but to win that weekend. She wrote an entry fee check that she could not cash and entered three events. I suspected that someone was watching over us, but I could not put a finger on just who it was that put that miracle together.

It was a common occurrence when things just seemed to work out. I had constant right side abdomen pain and my parents constantly rushed me to the hospital, worried that I might be taken the same way my dad's sister passed as her appendix burst. The hospital would generally turn my parents around and send them home as paranoid parents. Fifteen years later, my appendix was still an issue. I fainted while walking down the main street of Peterborough while shopping alone. I remember my teeth hitting the paved sidewalk. A lady walking behind me came to my aid and helped me up, and in my visual blindness, I could see a white object passing on the road in front of me. I waved my hands and said that that was my mother driving by, and the woman waved my mother down at that moment and I was taken to the hospital. What are the odds that my mother was passing at the same time some lady was scraping me off the sidewalk? Plus, I was visually blinded by the pain and could only see a white blur. Odd happenings were normal for me. I began to believe in them.

Mom would often tell me to stop talking to myself but, the funny thing is, I was constantly babbling and talking to Jesus. I was constantly asking Him questions and wondering why I was given four children and a mother to look after. I loved it! I felt like I was made to do the job. I enjoyed all the responsibility and freedom it gave me. I loved all my sisters so very much. We were drawn to attend church. In the younger years, we attended Sunday school at times, but only when Mom could afford to put money on the church plate, and it became a place that answered some of the questions we had about Jesus. We learned some of the stories in the Bible and some of the passages, but there was no formal instruction that I can remember, probably because we never lived long enough in one place to form a solid biblical foundation or belief system.

Most of our friends at school had mothers and fathers, so we usually did not speak too much about our circumstances at home. Teachers did not recognize the fact that we never took lunches to school or that we would wear the same clothes repeatedly. I learned how to sew eventually, which gave a little variety to our outerwear. We always wondered if the neighbors ever noticed that the front curtains became shirts and pants and, at one point, bathing suits for the entire five of us. It's funny how creative you can be when money is in short supply.

Most of our time was spent at home alone while our mother was working the evening shift until about midnight. As we always lived far out in the country, it made our days long because the school bus rides were usually an hour each way, morning and evening. By the time we arrived home, had dinner and did homework, it was time for bed, and that routine would start over again the next morning. Mom later explained to us that she could never let us live in the city because we would not have been safe, especially with five girls alone. We learned to love the country and the great outdoors. When mom would take us out anywhere, she would always tell us to act like ladies and mind our manners.

When she was home, she tried to make us understand the importance of prayer before bed and the idea that sin was bad and that we needed to be kind to others and always treat people the way we wished to be treated. Essentially, we were all left in the hands of the world to raise, and I knew I needed to be strong like her and I knew I needed to do all I could to make her proud of me. But still, that Bible sat on the shelf. I would stare at it and wonder what secrets it held, and I only dreamed that someday I could unravel its mystery.

Chapter 4

HOLY BIBLE BREATHED BY GOD

The secret key that unlocks the Holy Bible is available to all of us, and that key would not be granted to me until I was "born again." The Bible states that man pens the pages, but

> **All scripture is inspired by God and is useful to teach us what is true and to make us realize what is wrong in our lives. It corrects us when we are wrong and teaches us to do what is right. God uses it to prepare and equip his people to do every good work. (2 Timothy 3:16–17 NLT)**

The Bible is precious, and all that is written is true and accurate to the minute. It is both the history and the prophecy of humanity, as it was written long before each fulfillment of events was foretold. More importantly, its stories are revealed by people who witnessed these events in real time, and many witnesses repeated the same stories, as the apostle Peter reveals in his letter,

> **For we were not making up clever stories when we told you about the powerful coming of our Lord Jesus Christ. We saw his majestic splendor with our own eyes. (2 Peter 1:16 NLT)**

God breathed out sixty-six (books) chapters through forty different authors, written by eyewitnesses over a period of fifteen hundred years, as confirmed by over twenty-three thousand archeological digs. The Bible is a supernatural book that reveals the past, the present, and the future of mankind and, most importantly, it is our guidebook for life that shows the right way to live. It teaches us who God is and how to discern His voice when he speaks to us. Our Father in heaven reminds us,

> **I will guide you along the best pathway for your life. I will advise you and watch over you. (Psalm 32:8 NLT)**

> **For the word of God is alive and powerful. It is sharper than the sharpest two-edged sword, cutting between soul and spirit., between joint and marrow. It exposes our innermost thoughts and desires. (Hebrews 4:12 NLT)**

Today, I know the Word of God is alive and, the more I read and reread it, the closer I get to its spiritual author.

Oddly enough, the Bible has far outsold any other book, yet it stands on shelves unread and—even more importantly—less understood. History has revealed times when the Bible was not allowed in the hands of the commoner and if those people were caught with it, they were jailed or killed. There was a time when the books were burned, and some even tried to change certain editions to change the meanings. Most are copied directly from the original manuscripts and, with the discovery of the Dead Sea Scrolls, they are still passed word for word through many generations. God is mighty and He always finds a way to keep His Word pure and available to all who seek it. The evil one has used tricks and misinformation to keep society from having an interest in understanding its depth, and some interpretations have been twisted to deceive its followers. It's time to open its pages, read scripture for myself, and know the Word firsthand.

Chapter 5

CLARITY IN READING THE INSTRUCTIONS

As determined as I am to become better versed in explaining myself, another sinking feeling came over me: how do I do justice to such a critical part of one's life? This was the most important step in my entire existence, period. I cannot emphasize that enough. It truly is the beginning of who I really am. I almost cry when I think I could have experienced being "born again" sooner. When I finally understood the magnitude and glory of this life event, I wanted to kick myself for not listening to others when they tried telling me about being "born again."

My thoughts drift back to my sister with the Bible gift; her response should not have surprised me as I can remember rolling my eyes when one of my friends told me that the enemy was responsible for my blindness. "Enemy? What enemy?" I questioned. I had no clue back then. Most people do not even think there is an evil force opposing all that they do. Clarity comes with the experience of doing, but wisdom is gained through the ages and that information is written down for others to not repeat. Just like instruction manuals, generally they are provided with each product purchase.

Personally, I used to toss them out and tackle the task on my own accord. Most times, after an unsuccessful assembly, I would have to go through the garbage to fish them out. The owner's manual gives you a complete overview of the entire process, from start to finish. Surprisingly, I found other benefits, such as what the product could do for me above and beyond my expectations, which I would have missed without reading the manual. It's heart-wrenching how we sometimes fail to learn from history or others' experiences. And the biblical scriptures are no different—an owner's manual like NO OTHER.

Chapter 6

THE HOLE IN THE CENTER OF MY HEART

Let me begin with something I have felt since childhood. I am going to call it an empty hole in the center of my heart for lack of a better way of describing it. I probably cannot remember a time when I did not have that utter emptiness. I look back at my childhood as a happy time of independence and freedom, and I believe that this empty feeling stems from something greater and more divine in nature. Over time, this hole grew larger and larger. I have spent my entire life trying to fill it and, when that didn't work, I tried to ignore it using some form of distraction.

I now see that most people must have it as well as I observe most folks consumed with the same distractions: cell phones, money, fame, addiction, work, sex, television, and countless other things. I tried to fill this empty hole with the accumulation of money, alcohol addiction, and obsessive career success. At times, this emptiness would weigh me down with such profound sadness. I think we all reach a point where we start to think about our lives, our destiny, and our choices, and we begin looking inside ourselves for answers. I began by listening to a small voice inside my head, one I often ignored, and I began to be drawn to the unfamiliar.

I was drawn to the New-Age agenda and the world of spiritualism. God sometimes takes you to the opposite edge of the spectrum so you can be propelled back into the right position. I was fascinated by it. I learned yoga, meditation, Reiki healing, and spiritual mediumship. I met people who talked to the dead, and I was indoctrinated into a world of spirits that gave meaning to all things. I read into everything I did, which meant that even the animals around us brought issues and insight. I was given messages from great mystics that reiterated my past as if they were reading from my private diary. How could this not be the answer? I was told that I was "Joan of Arc" in a past life and that I died shouting our Lord's name, "Jesus! Jesus! Jesus!" And I was also told by mediums that the man I was dating in this life was the English soldier who brought me the cross that I had requested before my death. I was burned at the stake for heresy—the date, May 30, 1431.

How romantic and exciting it all seemed to be. I decided to take spiritualism to new levels and I was about to return to school to study spiritualism and become a Reverend in the faith. I knew the teacher who taught the courses and the training, and he was very excited that I was prepared to move forward in my studies. Somewhere along the line it went from feeling right to feeling wrong. I started making excuses. The decision to become a Spiritualist Reverend did not bring me peace, and I was feeling agitated. I noticed that the hole I thought was being filled still felt empty.

Moments before the course sign-up, I heard a voice say quite clearly in my mind, "You are heading in the wrong direction." It was not a verbal voice; it was almost like a visual thought. It was a nice voice, gentle and not forceful or sarcastic, but loving. I decided not to move forward with the courses and started backing away from the faith. I had thought God was central to the spiritualist faith but, as I pulled away from it, I started to feel better and better about my decision. The practicing mediums were getting answers to all sorts of life's questions, but these answers were coming from loved ones who had passed away. If they did not have the right answers when they were alive, how could they have better answers when they were dead? I often wondered what the Bible said about sorcery and speaking to the dead, but I never had the courage to look it up until now, when I found it in Deuteronomy.

> **Do not let your people practice fortune-telling, or use sorcery, or interpret omens, or engage in witchcraft, or cast spells, or function as mediums or psychics, or call forth the spirits of the dead. Anyone who does these things is detestable to the LORD. It is because the other nations have done these detestable things that the LORD your God will drive them out ahead of you. (Deuteronomy 18:10–12 NLT)**

There is no mistake here about what is right and what is wrong. Confusion was the meal of the day, to say the least. The gallant soldier who handed me the two sticks tied together to make the cross at my burning turned out to be a huge evil force in my life, and I woke up from that nightmare and walked away. As for Joan of Arc, her influence gave me a greater appetite and yearning to hear the voice of God. Even though the enemy tried to take me away from God by showing me something that seemed real and exciting, deep down, I could feel it was wrong. I left that life and turned away from its beliefs, knowing there was something special pulling me toward it.

Chapter 7

HEARING THE VOICE OF GOD

I sat in nowhere self-pity land for a few weeks, trying to hear instructions from that voice that had led me out of danger. Nothing, absolutely nothing. As time went on, I would get strange coincidences and happenings: a bible verse would show up repeatedly for me. A friend I had known for years had changed something in her life, and she mentioned Jesus, and then an invitation came along to attend church that would unknowingly change the trajectory of the rest of my life. I now understand that God whispers to His children, and it's up to us if we want to hear His voice. This is reinforced in a part of the Bible called Proverbs.

> **I called you so often, but you wouldn't come. I reached out to you, but you paid no attention. (Proverbs 1:24 NLT)**

God showed me the way by leaving good memories in unexpected places.

One of the best days of my life was when I invited my daughter, Victoria, to attend an event where the speaker was Phan Thi Kim Phuc. The napalm girl who is the South Vietnamese–born Canadian woman best known as the nine-year-old child depicted in the famous photograph taken on June 8, 1972, during the Vietnam War (referenced from Wikipedia). Kim is my heroine, and the famous photograph of her running naked and burning from napalm gas helped end the Vietnam War. Kim has since moved to Canada, and she is a motivational speaker and a warrior for peace. My daughter, Victoria, was fifteen years old at the time when I asked her to join me to listen to Kim speak. I was overjoyed to have her hear the story from such a strong and influential woman. We both sat on the edge of our seats, listening to Kim talk about her life and how she was able to turn something so horrible into something so beautiful. That event was held at The Embassy Church.

It would be eleven years later, when dating my now-husband Derreck, when he asked me in my time of self-pity to join him to attend worship service at The Embassy Church. I jumped at the chance to revisit this once-beautiful memory and I never expected what would soon transpire. Spiritually, I felt completely lost which put me in a state of complete limbo. I love that word; it gives absolutely no meaning to anything. I now know God puts us in limbo at times just to allow the noise of the world to be silenced so we can hear His voice.

Be still, and know that I am God! (Psalm 46:10 NLT)

I sure was not disappointed with my visit back to that Taunton Road church. Derreck and I arrived just as the service began and were seated in the last row in front of the sound stage. It's a big church, as it holds over twenty-five hundred people and we could not see the stage very well. It did not matter to me where we sat, as we were thrilled to attend church together for the first time, even though I felt like a fish out of water in this setting. During the sermon, the pastor mentioned that he had a message from the Lord for a certain couple in the congregation. It piqued my curiosity. Was it possible to hear God's voice? We had only been dating for a short time, and we were already falling in love.

As it goes, we were the couple. He pointed at us, and I was blown away. Pastor Doug asked us to stand-up and to motion to him if we were one or two. We were so far away that it was hard to communicate, but he asked us to put up one or two fingers. Understanding that we were single, he proceeded to say that we would eventually be married. He went on to further explain that he got a prophesy from God and that God had highlighted us as soon as we arrived, and he had to release God's word over us.

Messages were something that I was accustomed to, but they were delivered to the congregation through mediums and they were the words spoken by the dead. I was surprised but more excited to confirm that pastors could communicate directly with God! It felt true, and it felt right, and it felt real.

The Bible says,

> **Long ago God spoke many times and in many ways to our ancestors through the prophets. (Hebrews 1:1 NLT)**

God reveals,

> **If there is a prophet among you, I, the Lord, would reveal myself in visions. I would speak to them in dreams. (Numbers 12:6 NLT)**

The fact that we were singled out in front of over a thousand people with an unbelievable prophecy the first time I attended this church was unthinkable and captivating. Pastor Doug went on to say that he could see us in a boat crossing a great sea and that we would experience crosswinds on our journey from one shore to the other. He also revealed that it would take supernatural powers to move us across that seaway. The pastor went on to explain that we would need to turn to Jesus to survive. People around us congratulated us on our prophecy, and they mentioned that the pastor seldom does this, and we were blessed to receive such a message. I was intrigued by the prophecy, and I was awakened to the big question, *Can I communicate with God? What if?* Furthermore, crosswinds meant trouble and I left church that day both excited and warned.

Chapter 8

BORN AGAIN IN SPIRIT

The Embassy Church became a weekly event and we began our journey learning more about God and salvation. Derreck and I were slowly learning how much God loved us. I toyed with the idea of free will and how God was allowing me to reject Him or accept Him. It was a matter of my choice.

> **Anyone who isn't with me opposes me, and anyone who isn't working with me is actually working against me. (Luke 11:23 NLT)**

From the beginning of time, understand that

> **God created human beings in his own image. In the image of God, he created them; male and female he created them. (Genesis 1:27 NLT)**

We are a creation of God and a child of God; therefore, God is our Father. He created me, and it was up to me to reach out and take part in His gift of salvation through grace. If you are a parent, you already have a good idea of how vast and extraordinary that love can be. As parents, we cannot demand our children love and honor us out of our love for them; it is their own choice.

But to all who believe him and accept him, he gave the right to become children of God. (John 1:12 NLT)

God was allowing me to make my way back to Him and back to knowing I am a child of His kingdom. Please don't miss this point. Imagine God as your Father! That reversed so much of how I think of God. A father is one who has great mercy and love. He picks us up when we fall, he encourages us to move forward, he loves us, and best of all, he never leaves us. Today, where evil has attacked the concept of family through the breaking of the father, this biblical explanation of what God is for me made my heart sing. I was about to have a true father.

Attending church regularly, reading scripture, and trying to do all the right things still did not fill that empty space within my heart. *What is it that I am still missing? How do I reach that tipping point where I can truly connect with God? Can I ever walk in His presence with a clarity that makes life exuberant, where miracles are a daily occurrence, and where people are healed by the touch of the Holy Spirit?* I was desperately searching, and I was feeling confident I was closing in on something spectacular. I am human and not God. I make mistakes, and I sin. Yes, all of that is true, unfortunately. How can I refrain from sin? In a world where most people sin, it is starting to become difficult to differentiate between what is sin and what is not sin.

So put to death the sinful, earthly things lurking within you. Have nothing to do with sexual immorality, impurity, lust, and evil desires. Don't be greedy, for a greedy person is an idolater, worshipping the thing of this world. (Colossians 3:5 NLT)

How does God help us move away from sin and want to have the desire to become moral and ethical humans? As the scriptures say,

"For everyone has sinned; we all fall short of God's glorious standard" (Romans 3:23 NLT)

I even break my own rules and promises to myself. Look at New Year's Eve resolutions for a good example of this, and how long do they last? Most people don't even make it to the end of January without breaking their own promises to themselves. I know how many times I have tried to keep those New Year's resolutions and failed. What is it that makes it easier to follow the rules of God and not be lured into evil's trap? I vow to be relentless in my search for answers. I knew I was close; I could almost taste it.

Remembering the words of my mother, I thought to turn to Romans for this answer. Apostle Paul states,

For the wages of sin is death, but the free gift of God is eternal life through Christ Jesus our Lord. (Romans 6:23 NLT)

The Bible makes it clear that if you sin, your punishment is death. We are righteous or unrighteous before God, and the road leads to eternal light or eternal darkness.

For God made Christ, who never sinned, to be the offering for our sin, so that we could be made right with God through Christ. (2 Corinthians 5:21 NLT)

Jesus never sinned. Humans cannot stop sinning. Christ changes our sin nature when He died and rose again on the cross. It matters who we team up with as we learn and grow, as it states in the verse below in a statement made by the Apostle Paul

Don't team up with those who are unbe-lievers. How can righteousness be a partner with wickedness? How can light live with darkness? (2 Corinthians 6:14 NLT)

Can you move from a sinful life to a sinless life? What is the process of being "born again"?

Going back to scripture, I found it in the New Testament in the Gospel of John, where an educated Jewish priest questions Jesus about eternal life. When speaking to Nicodemus, a Jewish religious leader, Jesus replied,

I tell you the truth, unless you are born again, you cannot see the Kingdom of God. (John 3:3 NLT)

This statement in the Bible hit me hard. Think about this statement for a moment. Nicodemus was a Pharisee at the time of Jesus and he knew and followed all the laws of God, but even he was not able to enter the kingdom of God unless he was "born again." I was stunned by the magnitude of this statement. What? A high priest who would not see eternal life—how could that be? I had to understand why. There is no way to return to our mother's womb. Jesus is explaining a supernatural birth that takes place the moment we embrace the magnitude of the sacrifice that He underwent for His children so that they can be born again spiritually through knowing and following Him. Jesus repeats Himself in John,

I assure you; no one can enter the Kingdom of God without being born of water and the Spirit. Humans can reproduce human life, but Holy Spirit gives birth to spiritual life.

So don't be surprised when I say, you must be born again. (John 3:5–6 NLT)

God is spiritual and, to be born again, we need to move to a spiritual level. This is not a physical event; it is one done in the spiritual realm. We must be born of God. There is a spiritual exchange that occurs the moment you accept the truth! Ezekiel lends insight into the process when he reveals,

Then I sprinkle clean water on you, and you will be clean. Your filth will be washed away, and you will no longer worship idols. And I give you a new heart, and I will put a new Spirit in you. I will take out your stony, stubborn heart and give you a tender, responsive heart. And I will put my Spirit in you so you will follow my decrees and be careful to obey my regulations. (Ezekiel 36:25–27 NLT)

Finally, Nicodemus is starting to understand that to be "born again" he must request a spiritual renewal whereby all sins are wiped clean and the infusion of the Holy Spirit of God is imbued into the new believer. Ezekiel reveals that by the washing of water, we can be clean; and through this, we take on a new heart and a new spirit. That's it! I am starting to understand! There is an exchange of the old spirit for the new Spirit of God. How do I get started? What's the first step? Who can be saved?

Chapter 9

FOLLOWING THE RULES TO GET TO HEAVEN?

The path to salvation is available to everyone! Why is there not a huge lineup? Digging deeper into the book of Matthew, God sadly predicts that people are lined up, but in the wrong line.

> **You can enter God's kingdom only through the narrow gate. The highway to hell is broad, and its gate is wide for the many who choose that way. But the gateway to life is very narrow and the road is difficult, and a few ever find it. (Matthew 7:13–14 NLT)**

I want to find that narrow gate! Why is God's kingdom path so difficult?

> **The law was guardian until Christ came; it protected us until we could be made right with God through faith. (Galatians 3:24 NLT)**

Faith is the key that fits into the lock to the gate, and most people fail to make that connection. Faith is built when we turn away from the flesh; we are drawn to a spiritual experience with God.

Spirit versus flesh—there is a difference. The Bible refers to flesh as our carnal desires,

> **When you follow the desires of your sinful nature, the results are very clear: sexual immorality, impurity, lustful pleasures, idolatry, sorcery, hostility, quarreling, jealousy, outbursts of anger, selfish ambition, dissension, division, envy, drunkenness, wild parties, and other sins like these. (Galatians 5:19–21 NLT)**

The flesh seeks bad things, and the spirit seeks good things. I think I might have started to figure this out.

Until I move from a fleshly level to a spiritual level with God, I will not see the eternal kingdom He has set aside for me in heaven. Jesus sums it up with a profound and familiar verse from the Bible,

> **For this is how God loved the world: He gave his one and only Son, so that everyone who believes in him will not perish but have eternal life. God sent his Son into the world not to judge the world, but to save the world through him. (John 3:16–17 NLT)**

Jesus paid humanity's debt of sin on the cross and, when we accept that fact, we are automatically clean and the process of sanctification begins. Being "born again" is the spiritual change that manifests the moment we believe in Jesus Christ. This is the act of giving yourself to Christ. And upon that belief, I am drawn to repent of my sins and vow to maintain an ongoing walk with Jesus Christ. Sin no longer holds its power over me. And because of that love, I want to please Him in all ways and follow His decrees and laws, which become a yearning rather than a chore. We no longer need the law. As Holy Spirit now gives us awareness and guidance in all things. We follow our new heart, which means we begin to see through the eyes of Christ Jesus. This leads us to want to follow his will rather than our own will. God loves us so much that He gave His only Son to pay the debt for our sin through His death on the cross. When you understand the sacrifice and the extent to which God has gone to redeem the heart of man, you will truly see his fatherly love as well. The decision to vow to love, honor, and obey Christ Jesus wipes all sins away. Grace and mercy are what God offers, which means we simply must ask to be saved.

Eternal life is in heaven, where only pure souls can enter its gates. That purity is only available because Jesus died on the cross to cancel out the sins of the world. I was starting to understand the concept of what Jesus was saying to this Pharisee, Nicodemus. I realized that following the laws of God did not guarantee my entrance to heaven; it is the relationship I have with His Son, Christ Jesus, that opens the door to eternal life. To get to where God is, I needed to get to know Jesus! This famous verse takes on more meaning as Jesus reveals,

**I am the way, the truth, and the life. No
one can come to the Father except through me.
(John 14:6 NLT)**

This verse says so much; Jesus really is the only way! But is it not enough to follow the rules and just be a good person? God could never deny me eternal life in heaven, or could He? Yes! He could, according to the scriptures. There is God's law, and there is religious law. Following Jesus is not a religion. The Pharisees and Sadducees, at the time of Jesus, were religious leaders who followed religious law and opposed Jesus. As a matter of fact, they did not even recognize the Son of God when He came upon this earth. Jesus makes it very clear and He states an essential truth,

**Not everyone who calls out to me, "Lord!
Lord!" will enter the Kingdom of Heaven. Only
those who actually do the will of my Father in
heaven will enter. On judgment day many will
say to me, "Lord! Lord! We prophesied in your**

**name and cast out demons in your name and
performed many miracles in your name." But
I will reply, "I never knew you. Get away from
me, you who break God's laws." (Matthew
7:21–23 NLT)**

This verse confused me at first, but it illustrates the fact that these religious priests, who knew the writings of Moses upside down and backward, enforced those laws on the people; however, they missed the entire point of these laws. These laws were the compass to understanding and knowing who God is. They failed to know God through his Word. They knew God only on a fleshly level; they never understood communicating with him on a spiritual level. Jesus waved them away because they did not even know him. I want Jesus to remember me when I call to Him, and it would be horrible if He waved me away from Him when the time came to be received at the gates of heaven. No wonder religion starts wars, and following Jesus starts love. What do I do to move from being a stranger to Jesus to having a relationship with Him? I decided to get to know our Lord and Savior. The process of becoming "born again" begins today.

I began to study holy scripture, especially the words spoken by Christ Jesus, which are sometimes found in red print in most Bibles. I nervously fumbled through prayer, fasted, attended church every Sunday, and even found a wonderful Bible study group. As I got to know Jesus, I noticed that the more I learned about His life, the more I fell in love with Him. He became real to me and someone I wanted to emulate. Sometimes, we take something so simple and turn it into a complex and complicated endeavor. Scripture reveals how easy it is to move toward salvation,

**If you openly declare that Jesus is Lord
and believe in your heart that God raised him
from the dead, you will be saved. (Romans
10:9 NLT)**

It's that simple—just a heartfelt vow to love and honor the Lord Jesus. A promise to give myself to him, and an urgent asking for grace and mercy in my journey to becoming more like Christ. I was ready to be "born again," and I wanted to walk alongside our Lord and Savior!

Pastor Leon led the sermon that Sunday. At the end of each sermon there was generally an altar call. This is a time for unbelievers to be "born again" in a public forum. That Sunday was my day. My arm shot up, almost like I was not attached to it. Nothing could have stopped me. Tears flooded down my cheeks as I accepted Christ Jesus into my life and my heart with a vow of commitment. Pastor Leon assisted me through the salvation prayer. This is a prayer that you say out loud to God when you decide to commit yourself to a relationship with our Lord Jesus. The Holy Spirit filled that empty place in my heart the moment I committed. The sensation was a phenomenon! Why had no one told me about this miracle that occurs the moment you pledge your heart to Jesus? That empty hole in the center of my heart disappeared that day. I was sealed by God and am now a new creation. Who could have figured out that God fits perfectly inside that place of emptiness?

We truly are the temple of God, as we carry His light within us. I had read that salvation would cause instant changes physically, mentally and spiritually but, until I experienced it myself, I would never have believed the overwhelming transformation. Since that beautiful day, others have shared with me their "born-again" moments; some felt cascades of spiritual energy, and others felt gushes of love flowing upon them during their vow. With me, I was at peace instantaneously.

Over time, actual pains in my neck and back disappeared, addictions wiped out, pent-up family resentment released, and anger vanished. I forgave my father, I released the need to be in control of every aspect of my life, and today I am expressing myself and my opinion without fear. That day, I handed my life to God, and through His Son, Jesus Christ, I will have eternal life in heaven.

Now my focus is to build that one-to-one relationship with our precious Lord Jesus Christ.

Chapter 10

RECEIVING HOLY SPIRIT

I can humbly say that the greatest misunderstood conception of all is the gift of the Holy Spirit. This is the key to the entire process of being "born again" and the connecting force to Jesus. Jesus conquered death after the crucifixion, He walked among the disciples, and then He descended to heaven to sit at the right hand of God, but before leaving, He promised his disciples,

> **But I will send you the Advocate—the Spirit of truth. He will come to you from the Father and will testify all about me. (John 15:26 NLT)**

How powerful is that? We need nothing more than the Spirit of truth to guide and lead us. Paul's letter to the Ephesians expands on what the Holy Spirit can do:

> **Throw off your old sinful nature and your former way of life, which is corrupted by lust and deception. Instead, let the Spirit renew your thoughts and attitudes. Put on your new nature, created to be like God—truly righteous and holy. (Ephesians 4:22–24 NLT)**

Being righteous and holy means you are moving toward being an extension of God on earth. He goes on to show how this is the light of God within:

> **For once you were full of darkness, but now you have light from the Lord. So, live as people of light! For this light within you produces only what is right and good and true. (Ephesians 5:8–9 NLT)**

The Holy Spirit guides all "born-again" believers along the path to righteousness. You are no longer alone. He strengthens us when we are weak and picks us up when we fall, and He yokes with us to help carry all the heavy burdens of life. Consult with the Holy Spirit in all that you do.

God once walked the earth with Adam and Eve but, because of man's sinful nature, He no longer lives among humans. God resides above heaven, and He wants to be connected to each one of us through his son, Christ Jesus. That connection is the Holy Spirit within us which is God inside of us. Having the Spirit of God live within my body is one of the most humbling things I have ever been able to experience. We are entrusted with His light, and now we have the Holy Spirit to lead in keeping our temple clean and free from sin.

The Holy Spirit not only guides us and comforts us but also gives us each a spiritual gift:

> **To one person the Spirit gives the ability to give wise advice; to another the same spirit gives a message of special knowledge. The same spirit gives great faith to another, and to someone else the one Spirit gives the gift of healing. He gives one person the power to perform miracles, and another the ability to prophesy. He gives someone the ability to discern whether a message is from the Spirit of God or from another spirit. Still another per-**

son is given the ability to speak in unknown languages, while another is given the ability to interpret what is being said. It is the one and only Spirit who distributes all these gifts. He alone decides which gift each person should have. (1 Corinthians 12:8–11 NLT)

The gift can be something you were born with that God enhances, or it may be a new gift given to you after your salvation. These are gifts that you use to lead more people toward salvation while you are living here on earth. As my faith strengthened, God gifted me as well. He gifted me with the ability to have great faith. I pray that the Holy Spirit sharpens my skills and allows me to use them to further the kingdom of God. Some people are given one gift, and others are given more; it is the responsibility of the Holy Spirit to distribute each believer's gift.

Chapter 11

A JESUS-CENTERED LIFE

Now I am a "born-again" believer. My job is to witness and pass my testimony on to others. Most people are lost, and the lies of the world have left them broken and emotionally bankrupt, especially at this time when the pandemic has ended and now the rumors of control through climate change are bubbling up. Today, corruption is rampant, and the corporate elite march forward using righteous causes to masquerade their own unscrupulous agendas. Remember, Sadducees and Pharisees used religious law to oppress the masses, and now the corporate elite use climate change and scientific superiority to control today's populace. Nothing has changed. Folks today seem to be blind to the deception, and my hope is that they come to recognize that not all is what it appears to be. Failing that, attending church services tend to be the last thing on most people's minds. But when I ask people if they have ever experienced church, I find that they have some rather interesting observations because they lack knowledge and understanding of the process.

I guess the most repeated excuse I hear from people is the statement, "I used to go to church, and I read parts of scripture, but it did nothing for me." It's truly sad for me as it displays such a disconnect; I liken it to crossing a bridge where you are on the evil side and, when you are halfway across the bridge, you turn back, whereas if you went all the way to the other side, you would grasp the full effect.

Change does not occur until you receive the Holy Spirit. The Holy Spirit will not move into a dirty home. You cannot go halfway with salvation. It's all or nothing. You are human and you cannot do this alone. It's a gradual change that occurs in all parts of your life, not just on Sundays. Life changes the moment Jesus becomes first and when you focus on Him for the entire seven days of the week. I find that the more I try to walk in our Lord's footsteps, the more He reaches toward me. When I finally placed Jesus at the center, I expected signs, miracles and wonders to be the new normal. Remember, God knows you inside and out, so faking the "born-again" event is out of the question.

Faith is believing in something you cannot see. As echoed in the Bible,

> **Faith is the confidence that what we hope for will actually happen; it gives us assurance about things we cannot see. (Hebrews 11:1 NLT)**

When I realized that Jesus walked the earth, performed miracles, never sinned, died on the cross to cleanse our sins, was laid in a tomb, and rose from the dead after three days, I began to understand His love for His creation—man. Faith is a true knowing that all is meant for our good. The more faith you have, the more you can help change the world. Understanding that,

> **Once you were dead because of your disobedience and your many sins. You used to live in sin, just like the rest of the world, obeying the devil-the commander of the powers in the unseen world. He is the spirit at work in the hearts of those who refuse to obey God. (Ephesians 2:1–2 NLT)**

Paul talks about how we were dead before coming to Christ through spiritual birthing. He gives us a glimpse back at where we would be headed if we stayed in a life of disobedience and sin, and he highlights the fact that there is a spiritual battle on this earth. The Bible goes on to expand on what is causing all the deception and confusion in this world,

> **Satan, who is the god of this world, has blinded the minds of those that don't believe. They are unable to see the glorious light of the Good News. They don't understand this message about the glory of Christ, who is the exact likeness of God. (2 Corinthians 4:4 NLT)**

But there is hope, and the Scripture tells us,

> **But whenever someone turns to the Lord, the veil is taken away. (2 Corinthians 3:16 NLT)**

Satan is the god of this world. What? Now I am starting to see the depth of evil. Satan offered this world to Jesus during His forty-day fast in the desert, which I found in the Gospel of Matthew.

> **Next the devil took him to a very high mountain and showed him all the kingdoms of the world and their glory. "I will give it all to you," he said, "if you kneel down and worship me." "Get out of here, Satan," Jesus told him. "For the scriptures say, 'You must worship the Lord your God and serve only him.'" (Matthew 4:8–10 NLT)**

In the mighty exchange between Jesus and the devil, we are shown a demonstration of the power behind the living Word of God. Jesus rebukes Satan and then is attended to by His holy angels. Evil works hard to keep us all in the dark. Most people today listen to the devil but do not realize that a life with our Lord Jesus leads to the greatest wealth in all areas of their lives.

Jesus defines the true goal of Satan found in the Gospel of John.

The thief's purpose is to steal and kill and destroy. My purpose is to give them a rich and satisfying life. (John 10:10 NLT)

We should look forward to a rich and satisfying life because that was the purpose of the sacrifice that Jesus made on the cross. Yes, first for the forgiveness of sin, but Jesus beat death, poverty, illness, weakness, madness, sorrow, depression, regret, strife, demonic possession, addiction, and much more on that bittersweet day in history. Claim it because it is your invitation to accept. There is an enemy, which means there is an opposition! With that said, satanic forces are abound; Satan exists! Truly know that invisible and visible evil forces rule this earth. This huge evil force CANNOT be overcome on one's own accord. God warned us in Ephesians,

For we are not fighting against flesh-and-blood enemies, but against evil rulers and authorities of the unseen world, against mighty powers in this dark world, and against evil spirits in the heavenly places. (Ephesians 6:12 NLT)

There is truly a spiritual war going on, which originated in the time of Adam and Eve. Don't walk this earth alone, as you will be a child in a den of wolves. Take comfort in His partnership, and

For he will rescue you from every trap and protect you from deadly disease. He will cover you with his feathers. He will shelter you with his wings. His faithful promises are your armour and protection. (Psalm 91:3–4 NLT)

The words of this psalm are powerful and, when used in prayer, can make a big difference in times of loss or sadness. When in need,

> **the Lord hears his people when they call to him for help. He rescues them from all their troubles. The Lord is close to the broken hearted; he rescues those whose spirits are crushed. The righteous person faces many troubles, but the Lord comes to the rescue each time. For the Lord protects the bones of the righteous; not one of them is broken! Calamity will surely destroy the wicked, and those who hate the righteous will be punished. But the Lord will redeem those who serve him. No one who takes refuge in him will be condemned. (Psalm 34:17–22 NLT)**

Our cries are not in vain. We only need to voice them. This verse gives us great hope for the future of mankind. Being a believer means protection and comfort in times of grief and brokenness, and on the coming of judgment day, the righteous will be exempt.

Chapter 12

You Only Need to Ask

Salvation is given freely by God, and we only need to request it; it is not determined by our deeds.

> **God saved you by his grace when you believed. And you can't take credit for this; it is a gift from God. Salvation is not a reward for the good things we have done, so none of us can boast about it. (Ephesians 2:8–9 NLT)**

This is one of the most important concepts to comprehend in the Bible. God is saying that salvation is free for those who ask, no matter what you have said or done in the past. Divine grace is a gift from God.

> **Sin is no longer your master, for you no longer live under the requirements of the law. Instead, you live under the freedom of God's grace. (Romans 6:14 NLT)**

The idea of not having to follow the law is the most difficult idea in the Bible to really comprehend. I couldn't truly understand this idea until I realized that it is our true nature to sin and, when we are changed by the Holy Spirit, our nature also changes. We become dedicated to righteous living, and we are freed from the bonds of temptation and sin. These changes occur naturally and do not come from your strength, but from the power of God.

Holy Spirit will,

Get rid of all bitterness, rage, anger, harsh words, and slander, as well as all types of evil behaviour. (Ephesians 4:31 NLT)

Grace is why all those taking part in the process of being "born again" never get rejected by God the moment they give their lives to him. Grace is dispersed to all sinners from God from a place of full love and true generosity and, to get it, you only need to ask for it from a place of total belief. Grace is getting something in exchange for nothing.

As my life as a "born-again" believer grew, I looked forward to wonderful, unexpected events increasing, and they were revealed through connecting patterns, confirmations, visions, dreams, and miracles. I began to walk with Jesus in all that I did.

From the moment of my verbal confession, God reminded me,

And do not bring sorrow to God's Holy Spirit by the way you live. Remember, he has identified you as his own, guaranteeing that you will be saved on the day of redemption. (Ephesians 4:30 NLT)

I hope you are getting the idea! This is a process, but more importantly, being "born again" is an unforgettable event of moving from a fleshly existence to a spiritual connection, and it is an ongoing relationship with Christ Jesus. I really suggest learning as much as you can about the Lord Jesus before you step forward with your faith-filled vow.

May God give you more and more grace and peace as you grow in your knowledge of God and Jesus our Lord. (2 Peter 1:2 NLT)

Until you start knowing who He is and what God demands of us, stay at this level of understanding and only move forward when your heart grows with love for Him. Only then do I suggest that you confess your newfound truth and say your vow. Apostle Paul says it best in his letter to the Romans,

And so dear brothers and sisters, I plead with you to give your bodies to God because of all he has done for you. Let them be a living and holy sacrifice—the kind he will find acceptable. This is truly the way to worship him. Don't copy behaviours and customs of this world, but let God transform you into a new person by changing the way you think. (Romans 12:1–2 NLT)

Look forward to the new person you will become—the person you were born to become.

When you are ready, come to Jesus as you are and recognize that no one is ever turned away. He invites us to come with all our addictions, anger, greediness, anguish, guilt, illness, disease and fear. Allow the Holy Spirit to gain entrance to your heart and He will begin his work removing all negative traits. I have witnessed those who walk out of church after publicly announcing their faith, easily shedding their addictions after becoming sealed by the Holy Spirit. Some feel a whoosh of the Holy Spirit move from head to toe, and others feel great peace, but for most people, it's gradual, and changes happen slowly. The Holy Spirit takes its time to shape and sculpt each one of us. The veil is lifted, and now we will see the world in such a different way. The Holy Spirit strengthens us and serves as our communication beacon between Jesus and God.

> **But you have received the Holy Spirit, and he lives within you, so you don't need anyone to teach you what is true. For the Spirit teaches you everything you need to know, and what he teaches you is true-it is not a lie. (1 John 2:27 NLT)**

Lean on Him for all truth. As you move forward in your journey, remember to always consult the Holy Spirit in all that you do or say. Spend time in the Word and in prayer, and listen for the voice of God. Meditating on biblical text will eventually lead you to communication becoming a two-way street.

Chapter 13

THE ENEMY IS REAL

Most "born-again" believers are not warned about one thing when they transition to a spiritual birthing, and I wish to share this with you because this is what made the entire experience even more real for me. During the first eight months of my salvation, I was running into a string of what I called bad breaks. No, now looking back, they were disasters. I was fired without cause from my job, my daughter lost a baby in early pregnancy, bills were piling up, a diamond went missing, a generator almost blew up in the van, we had a gas leak at the house, appliances broke down, items went missing, I had flat tires, and many more odd happenings.

My husband and I started a new business and something was making our learning curve even steeper than it should be. We were doing jobs over two to three times to get them right and frustration began to set in. We felt that we made a mistake by buying a mobile auto painting restoration business. The final straw was drawn when after replacing a bad generator twice in our work van, my husband Derreck went to start the new one and it would not start. That day, we had already run into a few instances of cords coming unplugged and insects flying into our fresh paint job and now a third failed generator. We were both on the edge of our last nerve. This was not natural! Was this the crosswind that Pastor Doug had spoken about?

We finally realized that we were under demonic attack. We were confused. Should life not be smoother after you give your life to

Jesus? We packed up our jobsite that day and headed to the Embassy Church for advice. Pastor Rus took time to pray over us and he made us understand that any sin will open the doors to the enemy. We were not married yet, and he didn't force the issue, but he did say that living together was a sin.

A few weeks later, we were joined together in holy matrimony in the sight of God and all the pastors of our church. That was a door that the devil could no longer get to us through. Eight months of constant roadblocks were heartbreaking for us and rather frustrating. We had to figure out how to win against these attacks, as they kept coming. To all believers, Satan will come to call. The closer you move toward God, the more vigorously Satan tries to lure you back. Satan really hates when he loses a member of his club. Just like Jesus, you will be tested.

I heard God's voice one morning while praying for guidance on this issue, and He gave me one thought: "Take the authority that I have given you to defeat the devil." As believers, God gives us complete authority as we are heirs to his heavenly kingdom. Satan has no chance in this war. Fearlessly, I put on the full armor of God and stood up to Satan, verbally rebuking him from our home, our lives, and our business. It was me who did not see the strength that I now possess as a child of God and it was me who had to stand my ground against the devil. Things smoothed out. As a routine, each morning I continue to put on the full armor of God before I do anything else.

> **Putting on the belt of truth, and the body armour of God's righteousness. For shoes, put on the peace that comes from the Good News so that you will be fully prepared. In addition to all of these, hold up the shield of faith to stop the fiery arrows of the devil. Put on the salvation as your helmet, and take the sword of the Spirit, which is the word of God. (Ephesians 6:14–17 NLT)**

Events like what we survived frighten people back to their old lives after they become "born again" because they don't understand that the attacks are from Satan.

> **Stay alert! Watch out for your great enemy the devil. He prowls around like a roaring lion, looking for someone to devour. Stand firm against him and be strong in your faith. (1 Peter 5:8–9 NLT)**

The attacks were less frequent, but they kept coming. Pastor Brian from Selwyn Outreach Centre said a deliverance prayer over Derreck and me, and it took three weeks before I noticed that we were under total protection. I was overjoyed at this point. Don't give up. Ask others to pray for you during your time of transition, but be aware that you possess way more power than Satan when you team up with God. These attacks are genuine, and you will encounter the evil forces at work, but know that God is much bigger and much stronger, and you will need only to stand in the authority He has gifted you. You will be guided.

Chapter 14

PUSHING GOD OUT OF SOCIETY

The first humans failed to listen to God—remember Adam and Eve? We are all born without the Holy Spirit within us, which is why our nature is to sin. God gives us free will to choose our future existence as His children. Human behavior has given way to more and more corruption as each generation passes. With each generation, Satan seems to up the ante in corruptive forces, and people need more strength and faith to resist his temptations. I look back at my childhood and at television from then to now. We are programmed by television, and it has a huge influence on our choices and behavior. Here's a great example.

Between 1971 and 1974, there was a television sitcom called *The Dick Van Dyke Show,* which was a family comedy that featured a married couple. It was much like most shows that most families watched at the time. Television seldom featured nudity or violence, and profanity was seldom heard. In this television series, Rob and Laura Petrie were not allowed to be shown sleeping in one bed, even though they were married. When it was time to go to bed in the show, you would see them get into separate twin beds. What a contrast to today's programming. Anything goes today. Our children are exposed to so much violence and nudity through unsupervised television and cellular phone use, and long gone are the days of innocence and respect for one another and ourselves. Just watch an episode of *The Simpsons,* and you will get an idea of how far society has taken everything. It is a cartoon sitcom that features crude humor, bad parenting, disrespect for family members, and some degree of meanness.

These examples show the change in attitude from the '70s to now and how far society has deteriorated. When you turn to God, your sense of morality will change and your choices will be more positive. In the last few years, we have seen more evil in our world than ever, and most people have become desensitized, which leads to wanting more and more of the wrong things. Movies compete today in the categories of who has the most violent acts, authentic killings, and most nudity. These facts are truly shameful and disturbing.

By now, you truly understand the extent to which evil rules this world. People have forgotten the sanctity of marriage, the importance of family, and the honor of truth. Families are broken, and therefore, the children of broken homes lead broken lives, and then a generation is lost forever. Fathers have lost faith in themselves and have walked away from their responsibilities, leaving the family open to the wiles of the devil. Satan knows how to kill and destroy, and he has succeeded by attacking the family stronghold—fathers/husbands. Now evil is rampant, and good has been twisted to look like evil, and sin has been twisted to look like good. Today, children don't listen to their parents, people are rude to one another, and the elderly are locked away in homes after their so-called expiry date. Money has become the focus for most people and they will take advantage of others to accumulate wealth. The Bible talks about the end of days,

> **For people will love only themselves and their money. They will be boastful and proud, scoffing at God, disobedient to their parents and ungrateful. They will consider nothing sacred. They will be unloving and unforgiving; they will slander others and have no self-control. They will be cruel and hate what is good. They will betray their friends, be reckless. Be puffed up with pride, and love pleasure rather than God. (2 Timothy 3:2–4 NLT)**

Sound all too familiar? Hopefully, if not already, you will soon be a child of God, and the wrath that will come is kept from you. It is foretold,

> **Since we have been made right in God's sight by the blood of Christ, he will certainly save us from condemnation. (Romans 5:9 NLT)**

and repeated in Thessalonians,

> **For God chose to save us through our Lord Jesus, not to pour out his anger on us. (1 Thessalonians 5:9 NLT)**

I can't imagine what the wrath of God looks like. Probably best to not even try to imagine it.

Chapter 15

A New Creation

When you are ready to be unveiled, take the time and say the salvation prayer, and

Then God will give you a grand entrance into the eternal Kingdom of our Lord and Saviour Jesus Christ. (2 Peter 1:11 NLT)

I highly recommend you do this in a church or among believers, as

For where two or three gather together as my [God's] followers, I am [He is] there among them. (Matthew 18:20 NLT)

It is wonderful to have others around to celebrate, as this will be one of the most momentous events of your life. Most importantly, you do NOT need a church to accept Christ Jesus as your Savior. I recommend that you find other like-minded individuals to gather with, as the support from your brothers and sisters will help smooth out the transition and assist you in not backsliding in your journey. Know that it is good to join a church in order to grow in your faith and understanding of scripture. You will be drawn to church naturally.

In the Bible, all followers of Christ were baptized the moment they believed. With belief soon comes obedience—water baptism. The Holy Spirit will lead you to unite in Christ,

> **For you are all children of God through faith in Christ Jesus. And all who have been united with Christ in baptism have put on Christ, like putting on new clothes. There is no longer Jew or Gentile, slave or free, male or female. For you are all one in Christ Jesus. (Galatians 3:26–28 NLT)**

Today, we still follow the example of the saints. Baptism by water is a public declaration. Water baptism allows you to symbolically die to sin, submerged under water (the death of Jesus), while under water (Jesus in the tomb), and rise from the water, (Jesus beating death). You are well on your way to becoming a new creation with both the completion of your vow recognizing Jesus as your savior, and water baptism. My daughter, Victoria, was lucky enough to come to Jesus, over an Easter weekend, and receive water baptism all at the same time. Water baptism publicly declares your commitment to Christ Jesus.

In choosing a church you desire, make sure that the church that you attend preaches the Word of God and is not a false doctrine that does not have any resemblance to the words printed in the Bible. Jesus warns His disciples that there will be,

> **False Christs and false prophets that will arise and perform great signs and wonders so as to deceive, if possible, even God's chosen ones. (Matthew 24:24 NLT)**

Read and know your Bible and the Word of God so you can recognize false doctrine and teachings. Also, the Bible helps you to recognize the voice of the Holy Spirit in your life. The Holy Spirit speaks in words when you are meditating but more often through visions and dreams, and it is up to us to discern His voice. Scripture will also speak to you through the words while you are led to read certain passages along the route of learning. At the end of my testimony, there is an example of what you can say from your heart and in public or private when you decide to take the step toward being "born again." I call it the Salvation Prayer, otherwise known as the Sinner's Prayer. Remember that being "born again" is not a religion or a "cult"; it is a phrase that Jesus uses to describe the spiritual transformation that takes place while vowing to honor a personal relationship with him. When you perform this vow and put all your heart and soul into it, it is truly a supernatural event, and you will be changed forever. From that point on, you carry the light of God within your body. Your flesh nature dies to sin at that moment, and you will desire to live life without sin. Don't beat yourself up because you will make mistakes and loads of them. The difference is your intention changes. Holy Spirit will make you aware of your errors and redirect you. Transformation can be gradual as you go from being a sinner to moving toward being more Christlike. You will turn from what you want for yourself to what God wants for you, and you will notice a true feeling of inner peace and a profound need to love others.

Loving others is the pinnacle of the teaching of Christ Jesus. I found that I started seeing people through the eyes of God. I was seeing people for their good characteristics and not their flaws. The following is a blessing prayer that comes from the book of Numbers. The Lord asked Moses to pass on to Aaron and his sons to bless the children of Israel. I find it truly beautiful, and I often say it to others, and it makes me smile when others say it to me.

**May the Lord bless you and protect you.
May the Lord smile on you and be gracious to
you. May the Lord show you favour and give
you, his peace. (Numbers 6:24–26 NLT)**

We, as children of God, yearn to hear God's voice from heaven say the same words to us as were said to His Son, Jesus,

This is my dearly loved Son, who brings me great joy. (Matthew 3:17 NLT)

I am still relatively new in my learning, but what I find that seems to make sense is the fact that the more I soak in the scriptures and in prayer, the more I seem to hear from my Lord Jesus in heaven through the voice of the Holy Spirit. Come together with others in prayer, and let them confirm the messages that you get from the Holy Spirit. The voice of God is available! Always test the words that you hear, as God will confirm them with scripture, visions, dreams, or confirmation through others, before you move ahead on advice that you feel is from God.

I place Jesus at the center of all that I do, and at times, the Holy Spirit drops words or thoughts into my spirit, which is my most valued blessing to date. In the divine spiritual realm, belief comes first; then Jesus appears, which is confirmed in this statement:

Anything is possible if a person believes. (Mark 9:23 NLT)

Chapter 16

KEYS TO THE KINGDOM

This world is a battlefield where our souls are being waged between eternal life and eternal damnation. Satan seems to have the upper hand because he rules this world. Like all things, we all have a choice. You get to decide your future, as the Bible states,

You cannot drink from the cup of the Lord and from the cup of demons, too. You cannot eat at the Lord's table and at the table of demons, too. (1 Corinthians 10:21 NLT)

God's words may seem harsh, but they truly are not.

(God) is being patient for your sake. He does not want anyone to be destroyed but wants everyone to repent. (2 Peter 3:9 NLT)

Imagine a day when heaven truly is upon the earth.

And I saw the holy city, the new Jerusalem, coming down from God out of heaven like a bride beautifully dressed for her husband. (Revelation 21:2 NLT)

As a child of the Kingdom, I am granted an inheritance and the keys to His kingdom.

> **And I am certain that God, who began the good work within you, will continue his work until it is finally finished on the day when Christ Jesus returns. (Philippians 1:6 NLT)**

And when Jesus returns, it will be to retrieve His bride—those who are "born again." They will be safely taken to heaven while judgment is upon the world, something that is referred to as the rapture. Don't get too caught up in this concept as there is much controversy about God taking us up into heaven in the twinkling of an eye as it does not mention the word rapture in the Bible. But we do see many examples of this concept with people such as Enoch and Elijah. After judgment is complete, God will live among His believers on the new earth once again.

> **Look, God's home is now among his people! He will live with them, and they will be his people. God himself will be with them. He will wipe every tear from their eyes, and there will be no more death or sorrow or crying or pain. All these things are gone forever. (Revelation 21:3–4 NLT)**

In Revelation, the last book of the Bible, you will also find a full description of heaven and how glorious it will be. Here is a small excerpt of some of those verses where Jesus describes heaven,

> **The nations will walk in its light, and the kings of the world will enter the city in all their glory. Its gates will never be closed at the end of the day because there is no night there. And all the nations will bring Glory and honour into the city. Nothing evil will be allowed**

**to enter, nor anyone who practices shame-
ful idolatry and dishonesty—but only those
whose names are written in the Lamb's Book
of Life. (Revelation 21:24–27 NLT)**

Some glorify hell and make others think it's a more fascinating
place to spend their eternity, but please don't be fooled. I thank God
for His calling on my life, and I am overwhelmed with joy that He
did not give up on His calling on me. There is no mistake that you
have been led to my testimony. Hopefully you will connect with the
same emptiness that has sent me on the search for the only thing that
can fill that empty place in the center of my heart—Christ Jesus.

God is calling you today just by the fact that you are reading this
testimony. Know that your name is written in the Lamb's Book of
Life the moment you believe. Peace will come when you are officially
God's adopted child, an ambassador on earth, and a future citizen
of the kingdom of heaven. May God bless you, may His face shine
upon you, and may you—either Jew or Gentile—listen to Peter as he
commands believers shortly after the day of Pentecost with instructions that the Lord has left him with.

**Each of you must repent of your sins and
turn to God, and be baptized in the name of
Jesus Christ for the forgiveness of your sins.
Then you will receive the gift of the Holy Spirit.
This promise is to you, and to your children,
even to the Gentiles—all who have been called
by the Lord our God. (Acts 2:38–39 NLT)**

Chapter 17

THE FIGHT HAS JUST BEGUN

God took me on such a long tour, but I finally arrived at the destination of sweet salvation. Now my life is eternal, and I am destined to live in heaven after I pass from this world. But for now, my address is on earth. I am to abide by and help those brothers and sisters with support and comfort through faith. Life should not be difficult, but it is because the enemy has blinded the masses from reading the greatest manual of all; the Holy Bible. It took childhood poverty, parental divorce, teenage rebellion, college struggles, two failed marriages, and a miscarriage to make me just stop and think and listen to the most divine and powerful voice in all the galaxy—God. If you stand back and view all things from the vantage point of evil trying to wipe out good, it all comes into focus. God gave us that hole in our hearts because He knew we would search to fill it. It is the home for the Spirit of God. In a world of evil, we can only navigate it with God's compass to direct us; without it, we fall into the wrong hands.

This is where I come off the rails in understanding, but I don't want to leave you up in the air about what it means when I mention God in three persons. These three persons are the Father, the Son Jesus, and the Holy Spirit. This is where human understanding takes a back seat. All manifestations are God. Our God is immeasurable. We cannot even imagine properly the vast magnitude of his greatness. The Bible states that His Words created the heavens and the earth. Wow! Think about that statement for a moment. It proves one thing: He lives beyond both heaven and earth. He sees the beginning from the end and He lives in a world where a day is equal to a thousand years and a thousand years is equal to a day. I really don't think anyone has a solid grip on how incredible and magnificent our God really is from the perspective of humanity. My understanding through the Holy Spirit about the three persons of God is that they are equal parts that manifest in different ways so that God can relate to his children. God is holy and He appears in heaven among His twenty-four elders and His countless angels. God cannot be in the presence of sin, which means a soul cannot spiritually enter heaven without being born again. Heaven is a place of eternal life. God loves His children, and He needed to remove sin from them to give them the gift of eternal life in heaven. God had to come to earth in the form of man to offer Himself up as the last blood sacrifice for the forgiveness of sins, and that's where Jesus comes in.

Jesus is the earthly manifestation of God. He walked on earth as a man, died, and beat death to erase sin in man for those who believed and accepted His grace. Jesus explained to His disciples that they would receive the same power that raised Him from the dead ten days after He ascended into heaven to join His Father. Ten days later, called the day of Pentecost, all His believers experienced the miracle of the indwelling of the Holy Spirit.

Today, the moment you believe, you are imbued with that same power called the Holy Spirit. You carry God in your heart. The Holy Spirit fits perfectly inside that empty place inside your heart, and it is then that you feel true peace. Jesus confirmed that you can become even greater than He when you receive the Holy Spirit. Satan does not want you to know that you possess this power. If mankind understood this secret, then evil would not take root anywhere.

As a child of God, a believer in Christ, and one who houses the Holy Spirit within your body, you can now change the world. You are powerful! You are unstoppable! Fear no longer directs your life. Take authority from who you are in Christ Jesus. The Holy Spirit partners in directing your life, and when all Christian brothers and sisters move together as the Spirit of God flows like a river, we become a force that evil cannot withstand.

God wants us to recognize our position as His sons and daughters and, like Jacob in the Bible, he hungered to be blessed and exulted by Father God. Take authority over the power given to you. Jesus is the door that we open, the Holy Spirit is the guide that takes you to the door in purity and yearning, and it is God who gifts you with eternal life.

A Salvation Prayer

Heavenly Father, I come to Your throne in the name of Jesus Christ. It is written in Your word that if I confess with my mouth that Jesus is Lord and believe in my heart that You have raised Him from the dead, I shall be saved. I stand ready to be saved. I confess that I am a sinner. Forgive me, Lord, for all my sins. I repent, and I turn away from sin from this day forward. I believe that Jesus is Lord. He is the Lord of my life. Jesus died on the cross, was laid in a tomb for three days, and rose from the dead so that I might be saved. I accept the gift of forgiveness and grace. Today, You, Lord, fill that empty place in my heart with Your Holy Spirit. Fill me with the Holy Spirit. Thank You, Father God. I am overjoyed and truly humbled. I invite You, King Jesus, into my life through the Holy Spirit. I vow to worship You and grow in the knowledge of Your will for my life. I now know that my name is written in the Lamb's Book of Life, which means You have granted me eternal life in my home in the kingdom of heaven. In Jesus's mighty name. Amen.

Author's Note

One of the best ideas on how to change the direction of our planet came from the movie *Pay It Forward*, a 2000 American romantic drama film. The concept of the film is based on doing favors or good deeds for others and, rather than paying it back, they pay it forward. Trevor, the main character in the story, develops this plan to change the world and make it a better place for all people. Sadly, he dies before knowing that he has changed the world. This heartwarming tale has always helped me pay it forward in my life. It truly is the little things that we do for others that make all the differ-ence. If you felt this book led you one step closer to becoming born again, please pay it forward and give this book to someone you love. Or if you have a wonderful story to tell, I would love to hear from you in an email. You can find me at dnmahaney@yahoo.com. One hundred percent of the profits from the sale of this book will go to expand the Kingdom of God. I am truly grateful for your purchase.

About the Author

God uses the least of us to carry out His agenda and today He set His sights on Noanie Mahaney. Her love of writing and her newfound salvation explode in her Holy Spirit–inspired testimony, whereby she gives a greater understanding of the process of becoming "born again." Her master's degree hails from the kingdom of heaven, and her knowledge is the sword of the spirit, which is the Holy Bible. Noanie is a warrior of truth and freedom. God has given her marching orders to write about a subject that has lost understanding because society has become infiltrated by forces that have hidden the truth. God chose Noanie because she is ordinary. Just like you, she is a daughter, a sister, a mother, a wife, and a grandmother. She is a woman who sees the good in all those who step into her life, and she is a seeker and an overcomer. Noanie received salvation on February 17, 2019, and from that moment, the Lord inspired her to write about her experience so that all who are called will understand the true path to eternal life.